Jonathon Coudrille has also written and il
children of all ages, the highly acclaimed *'A I*
two *'Farmer Fisher'* books and *'Jumping Up*
The Vulgar Frog breaks entirely new groun
it has no words.

Published by Quartet Books Ltd/Solo Books
Members of the Namara Group
27-29 Goodge Street, London W1P 1FD

First Published 1983

British Library Cataloguing Publication Data

Coudrille, Jonathon

The Vulgar Frog

1. Frogs – Caricatures and cartoons

2. English wit and humor, Pictorial

I. Title

741.5'942 NC1749
ISBN 07043 34305

Printed and Bound by Mackays of Chatham Ltd., Kent.

The Vulgar Frog

Jonathon Coudrille

Pets, Young Frogs, Little Green Sons of
..............Well, Frogs

FROG

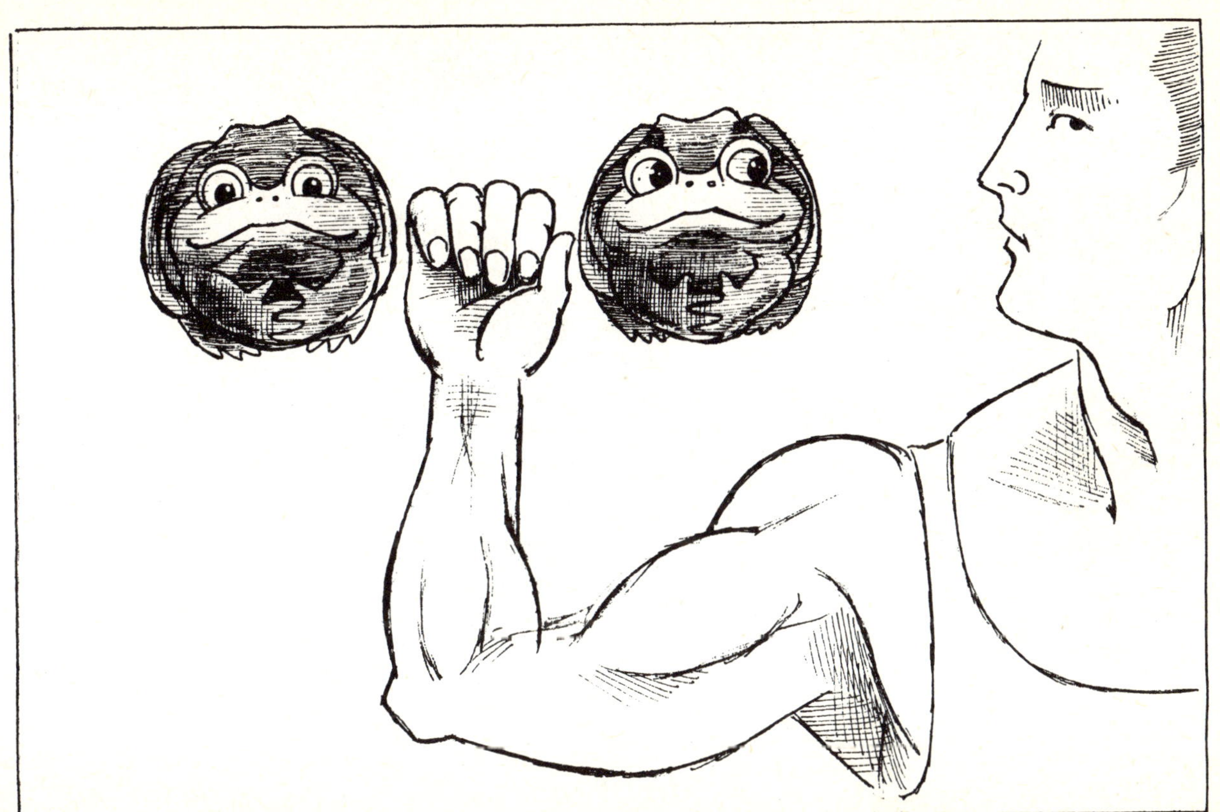

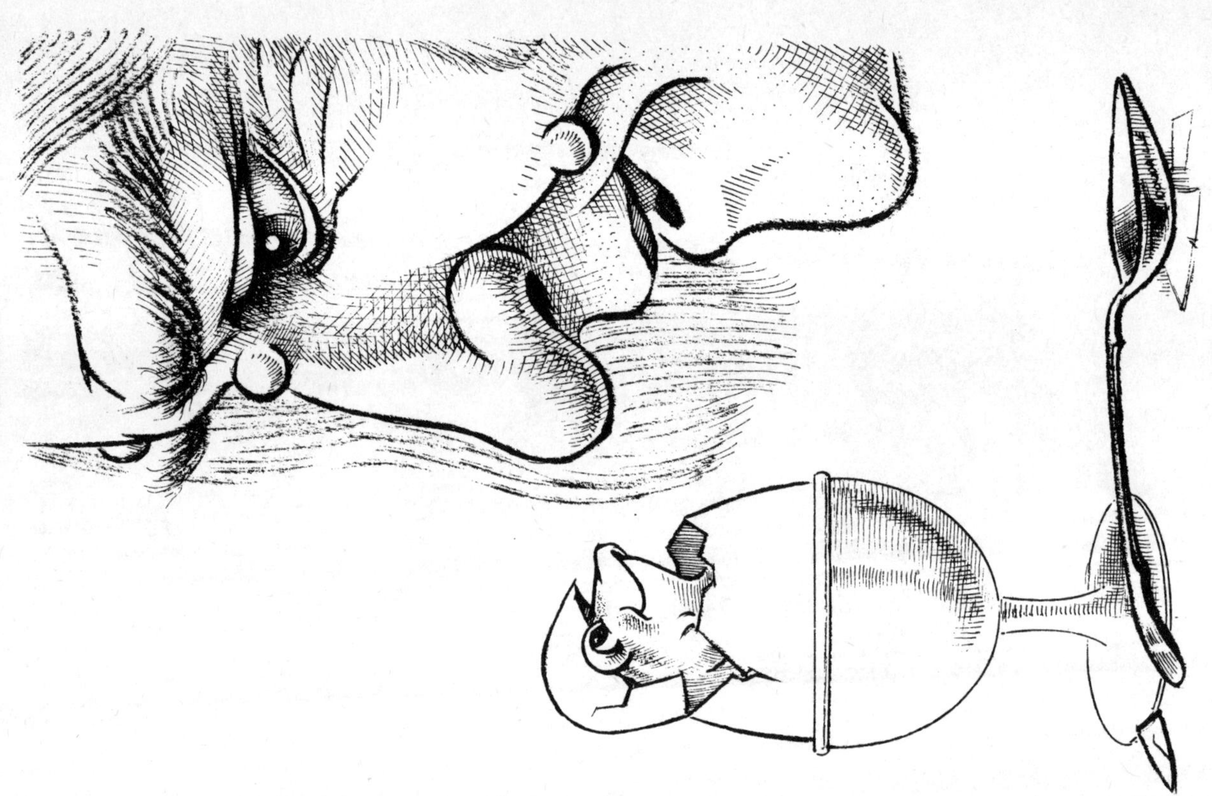

2+2 = 22
3+3 = 33
B. Pwog
form 4 c.
D

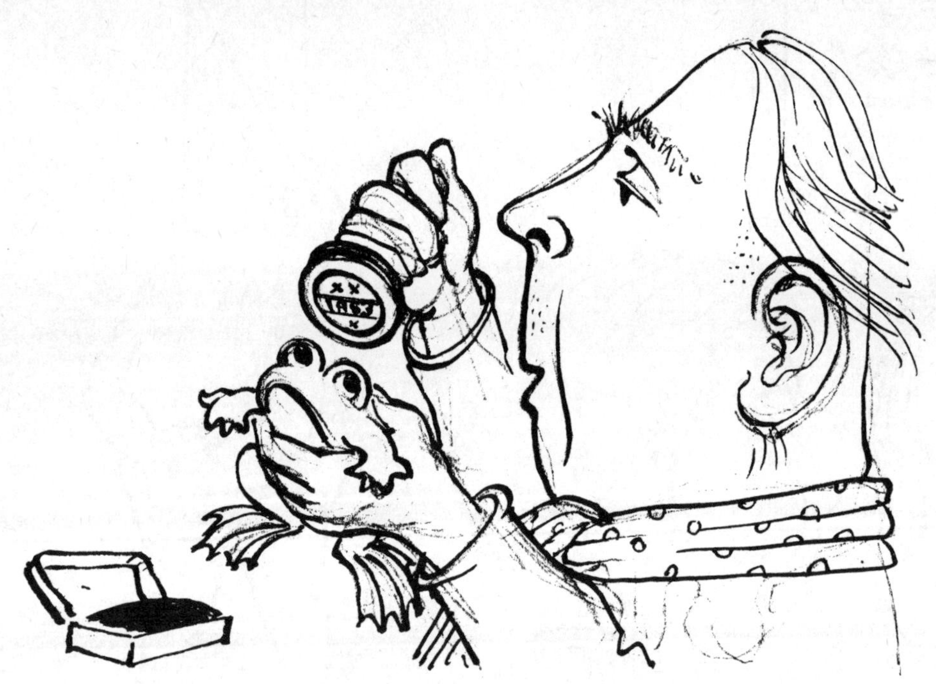

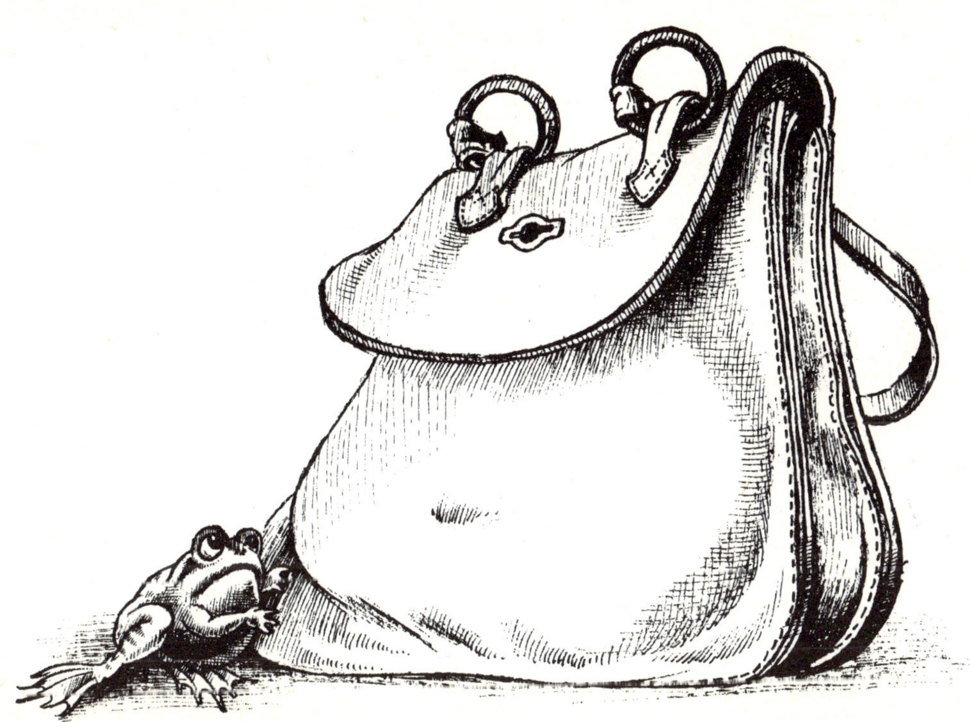

ANTHROPOMORPHISM

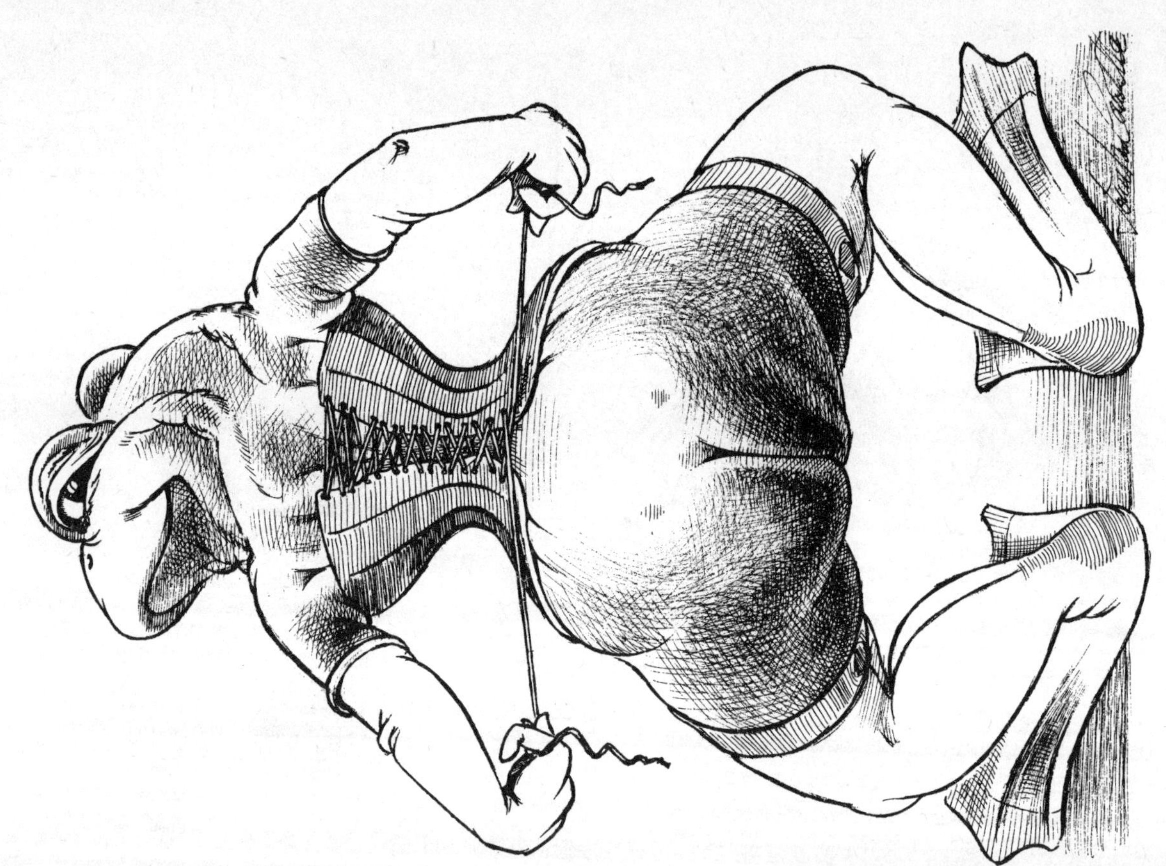

PUT MORE PAINT IN SPRAY
CLOSED FOR NOW
ONGAR
FANS EUPHORIC
FANTASTIC!
WONDERFUL.
'GREAT'
SAYS
MANAGER.
FAMINE
FLOOD
FIRE
'QUAKE
CRASH
RAPE
MURDER
POUND,
DOLLAR,
MARK,
YEN PLUNGE
WORSE TO COME
JUDGE RAPS LUNCH
WELL HELLO!
WORST DISASTER
EVER. MILLIONS
FEARED DEAD
"NASTY"
HOPE
RUNS OUT
CLASSIFIED.
GLAMOUR
WEAR.
COINS
RUBBER
SOCKS
ADULT
MOVIES
EARN
BIG
MONEY
CATASTROPHE
'UNPRECEDENTED'
UNIQUELY HORRIBLE
CIRCUMSTANCES,
EVEN WORSE
THAN PREVIOUSLY,
SAYS SPOKESMAN
AUTHORITIES
BLAMED.

MR. RANUS

MOTHER

Menu

ART, ARCHITECTURE AND PARANOIA

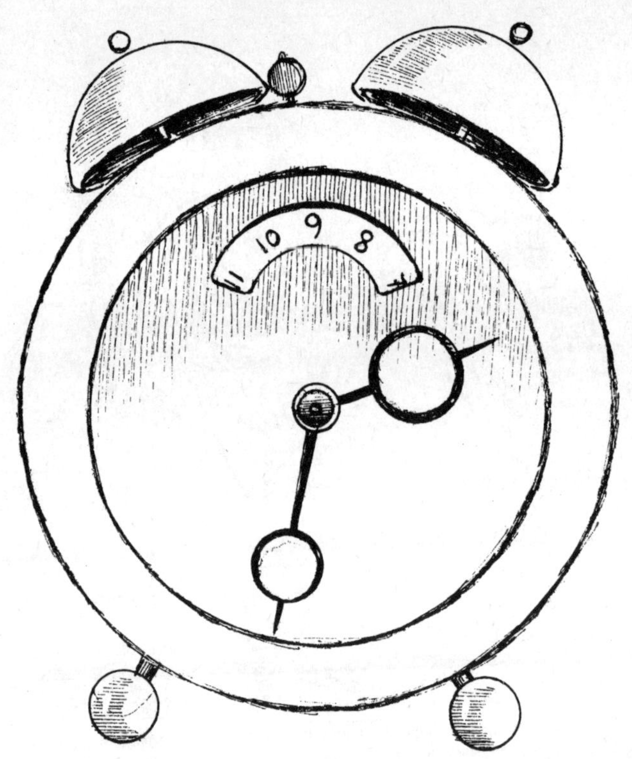
10 9 8

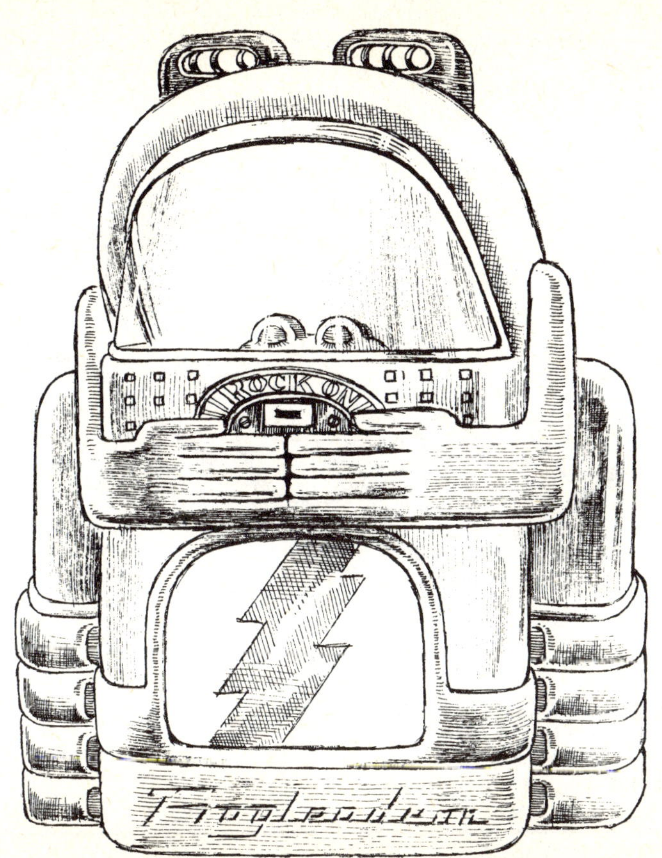
ROCK ON

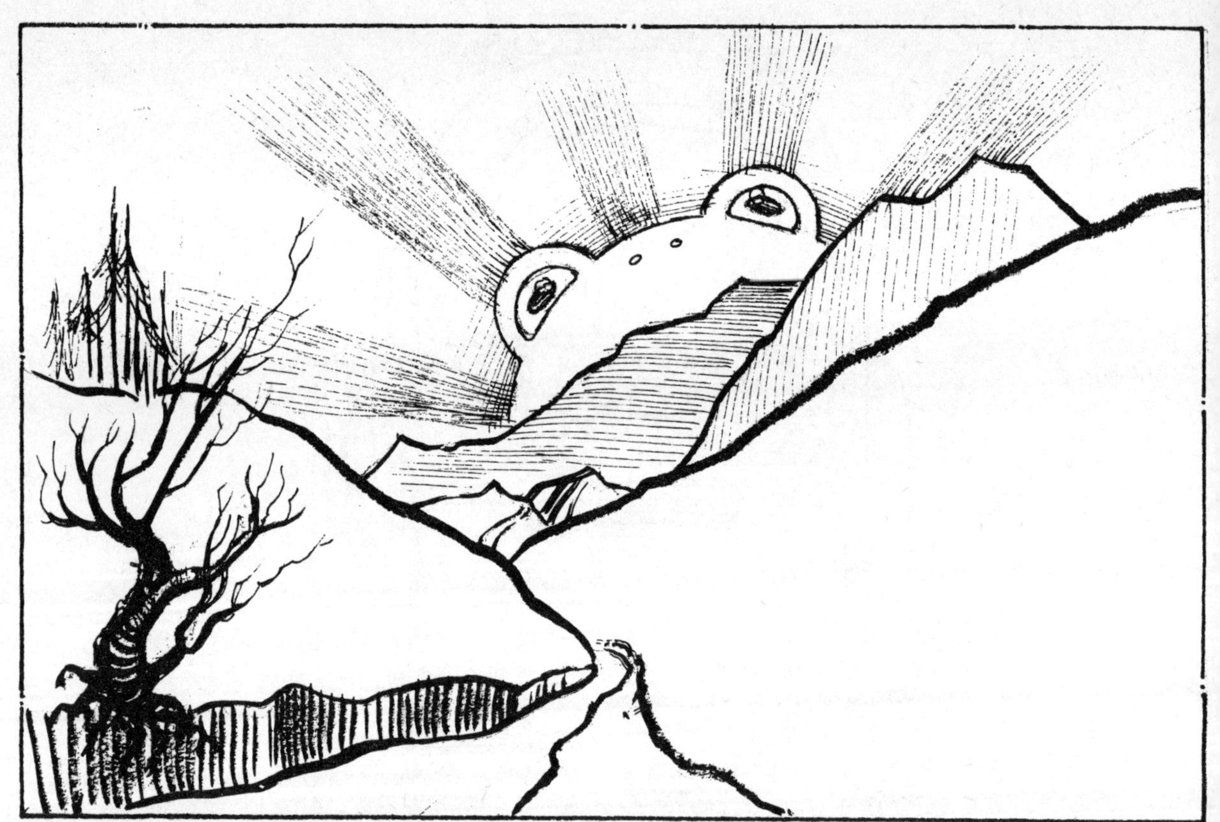

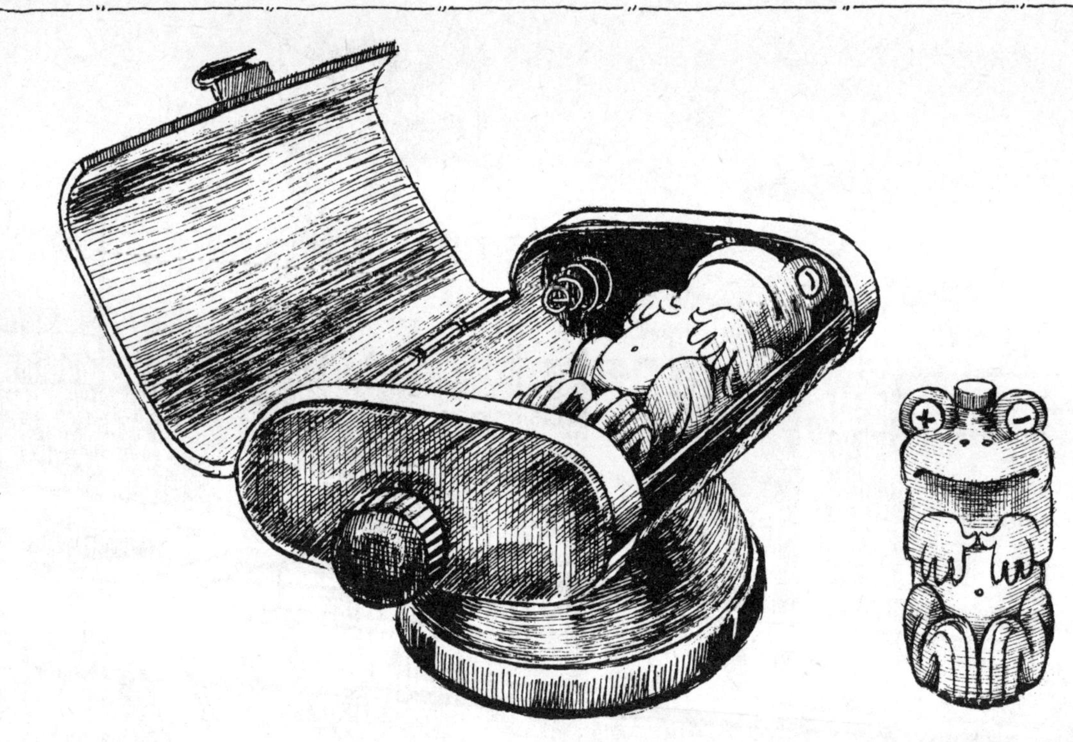

ON

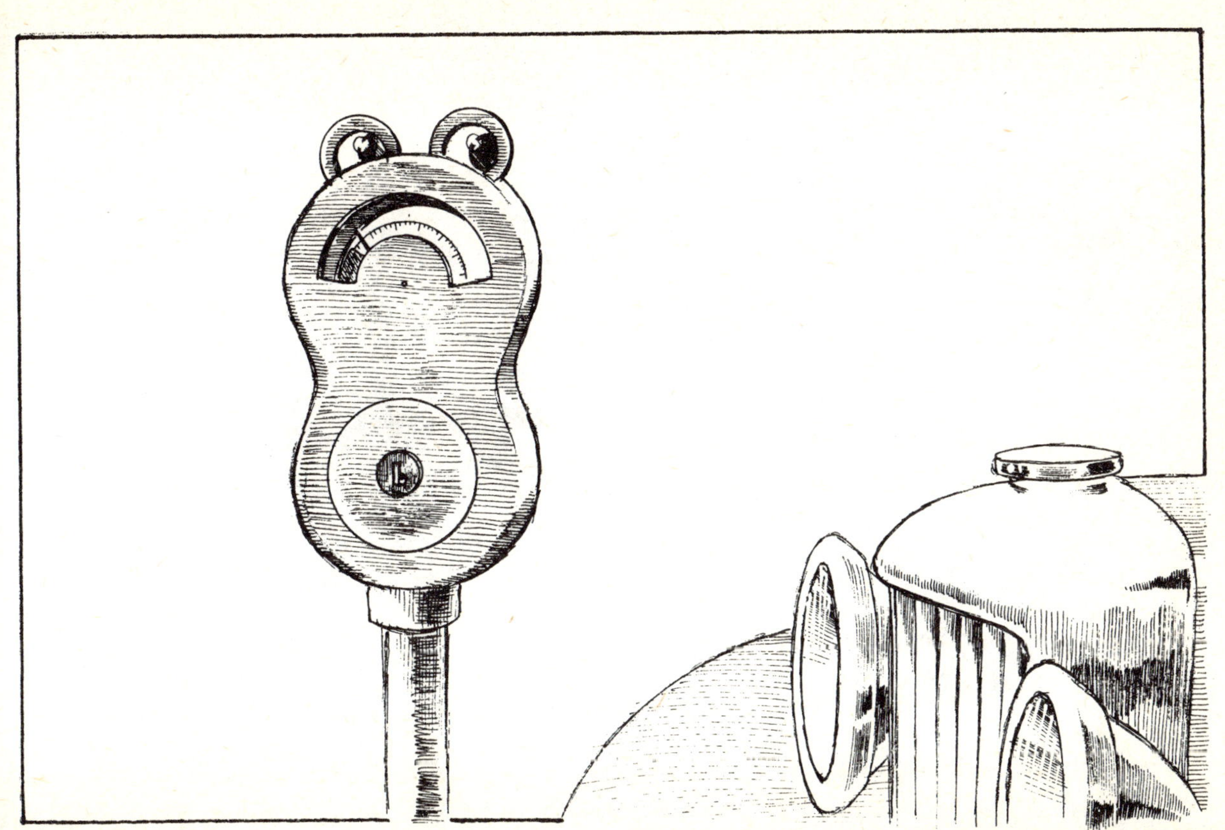

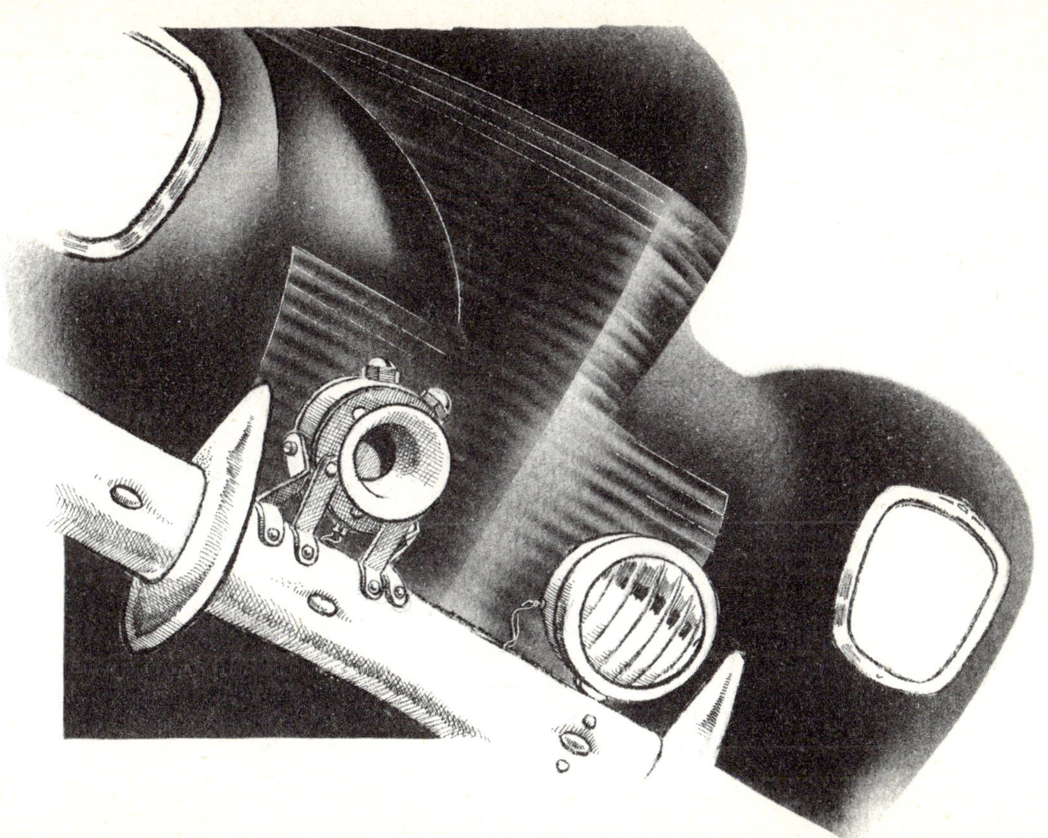

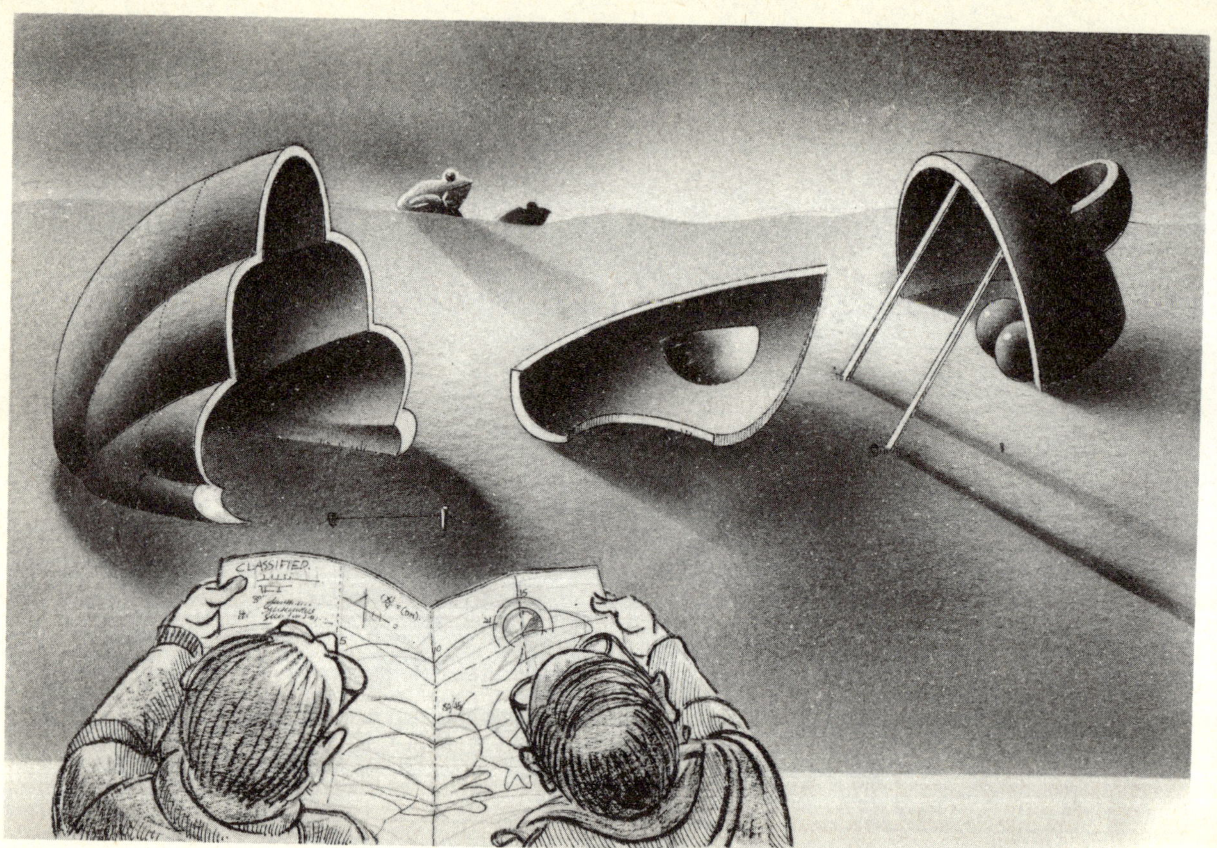
CLASSIFIED.

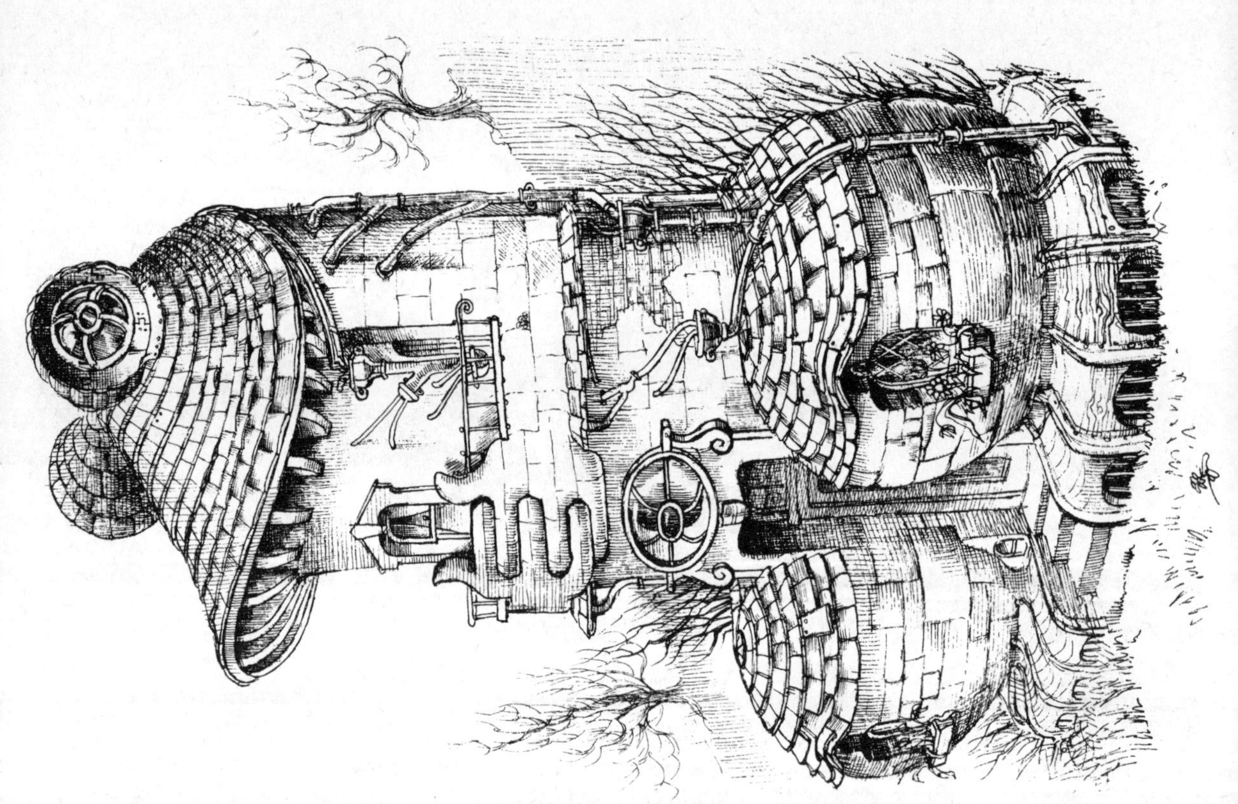

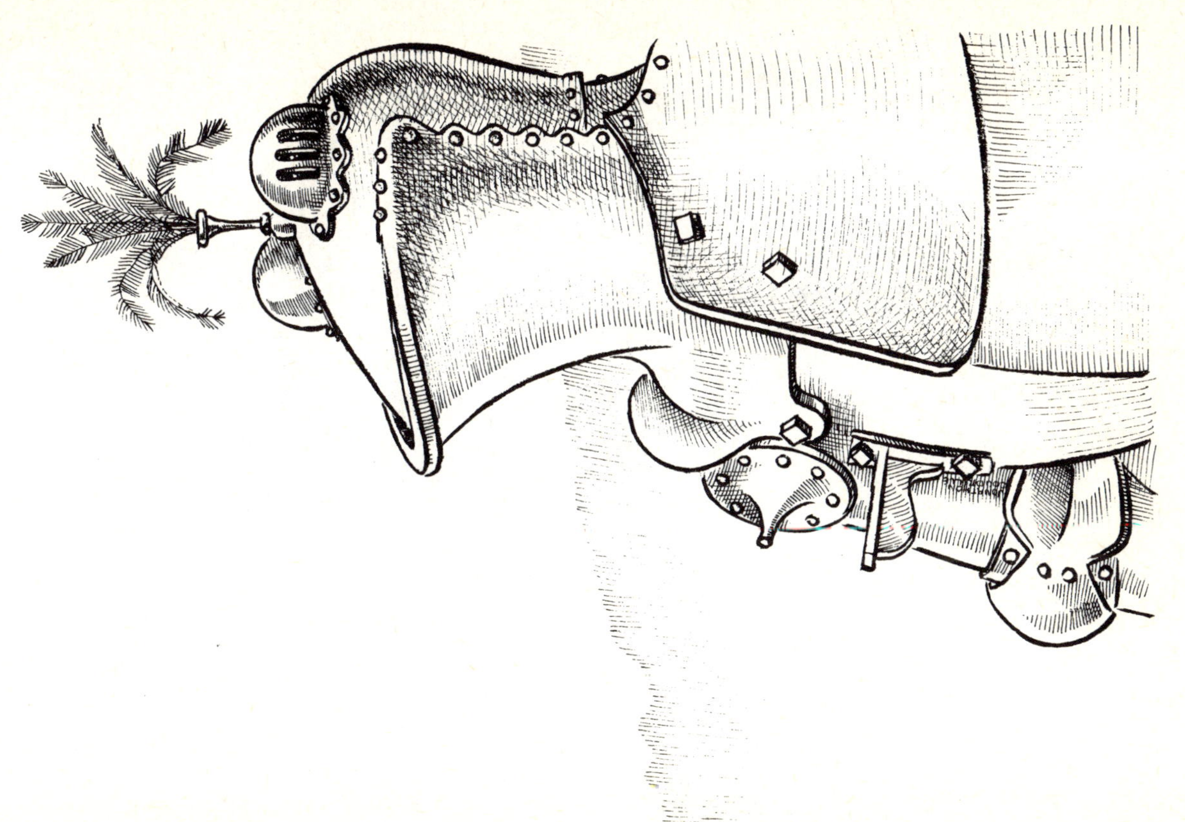

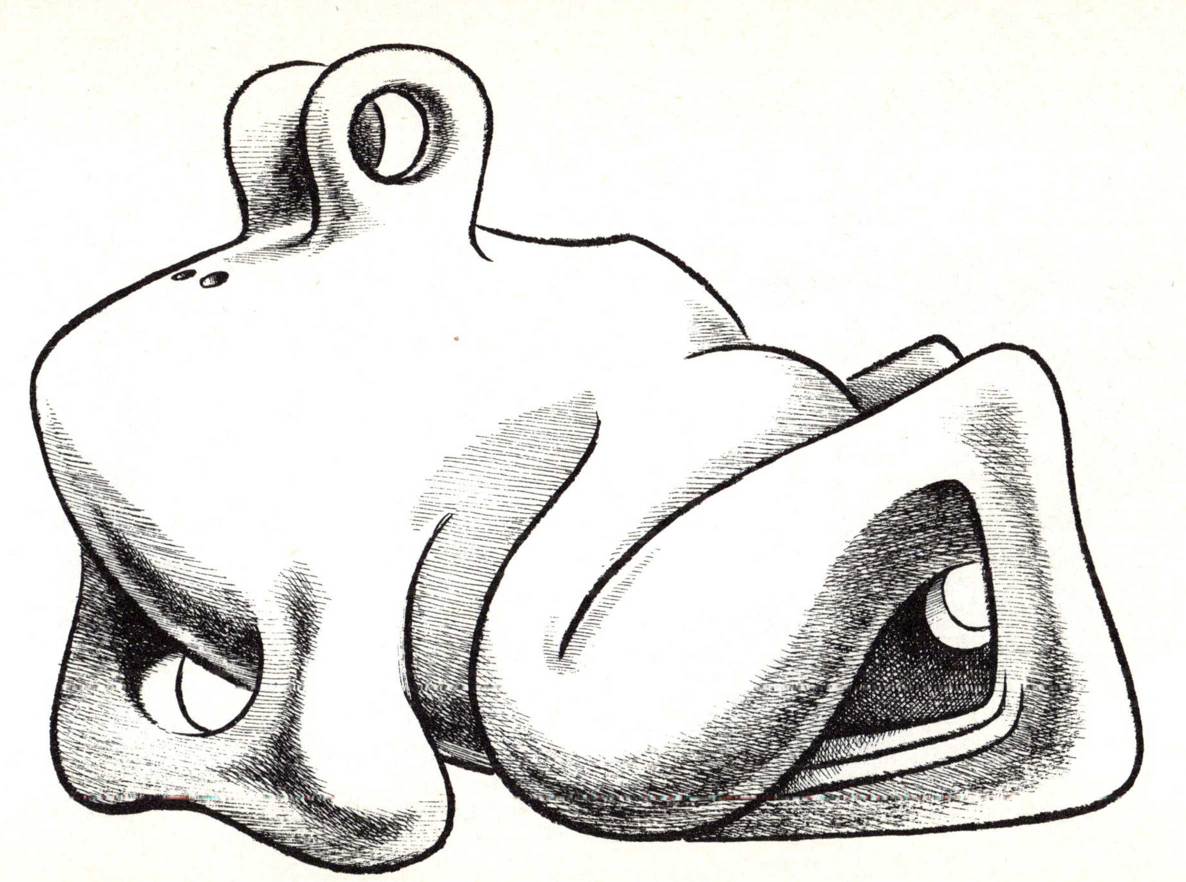

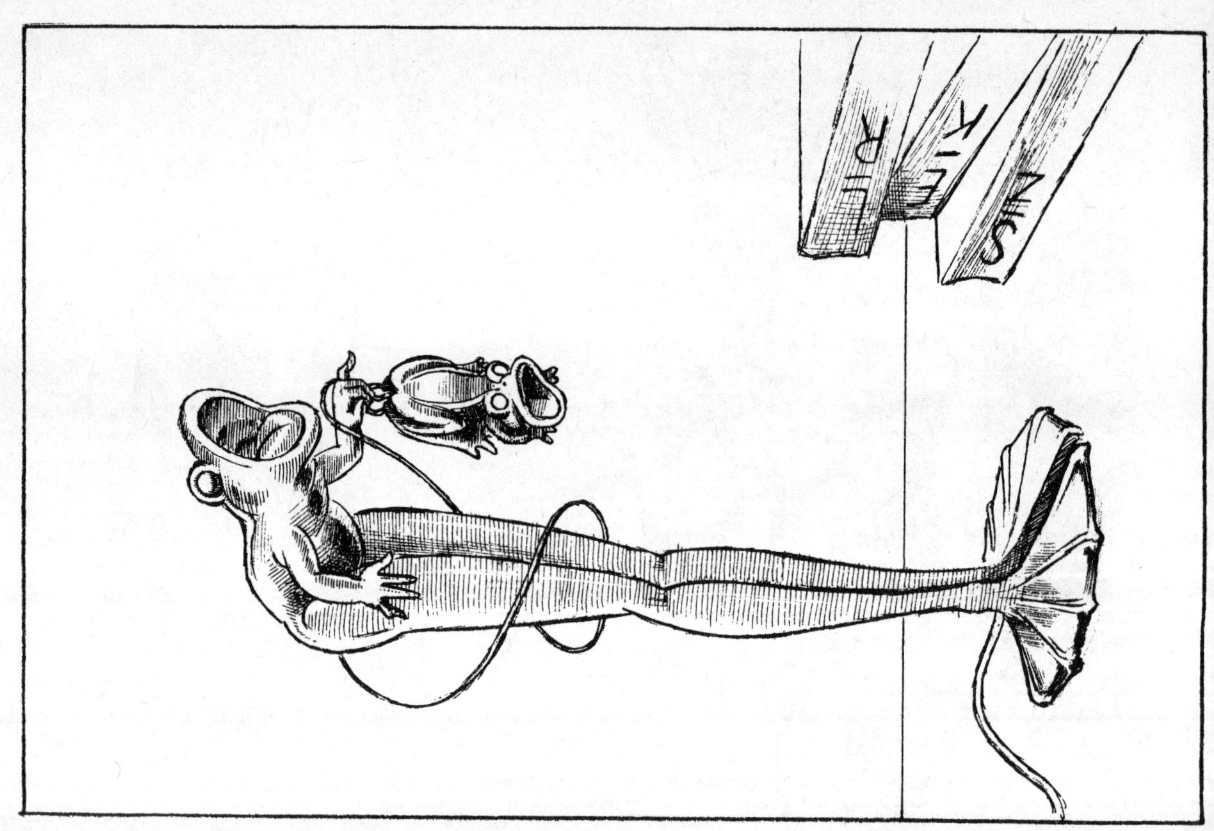

OPEN

A Green Comedy

THE
JUNIOR MONSOON
(REG) PAT 83214
ARCHITECTS RULE
AFC
I LIKE

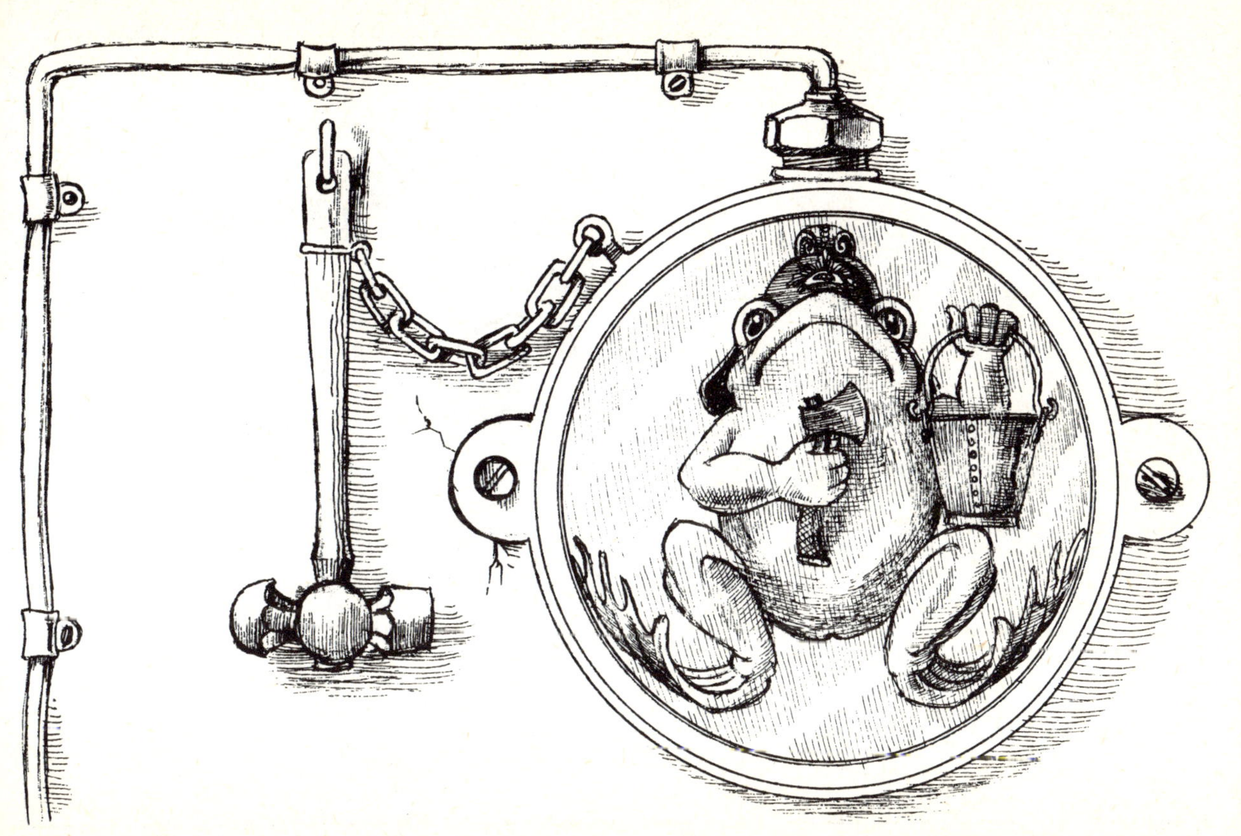

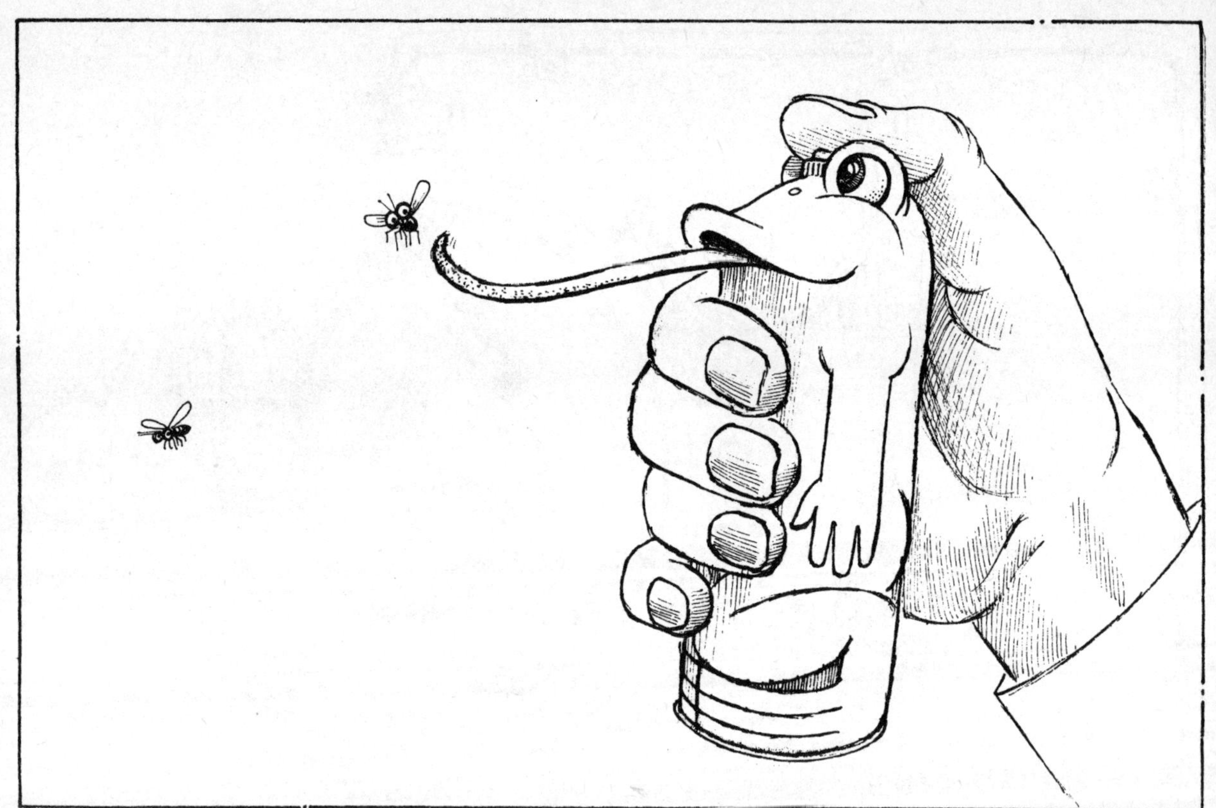

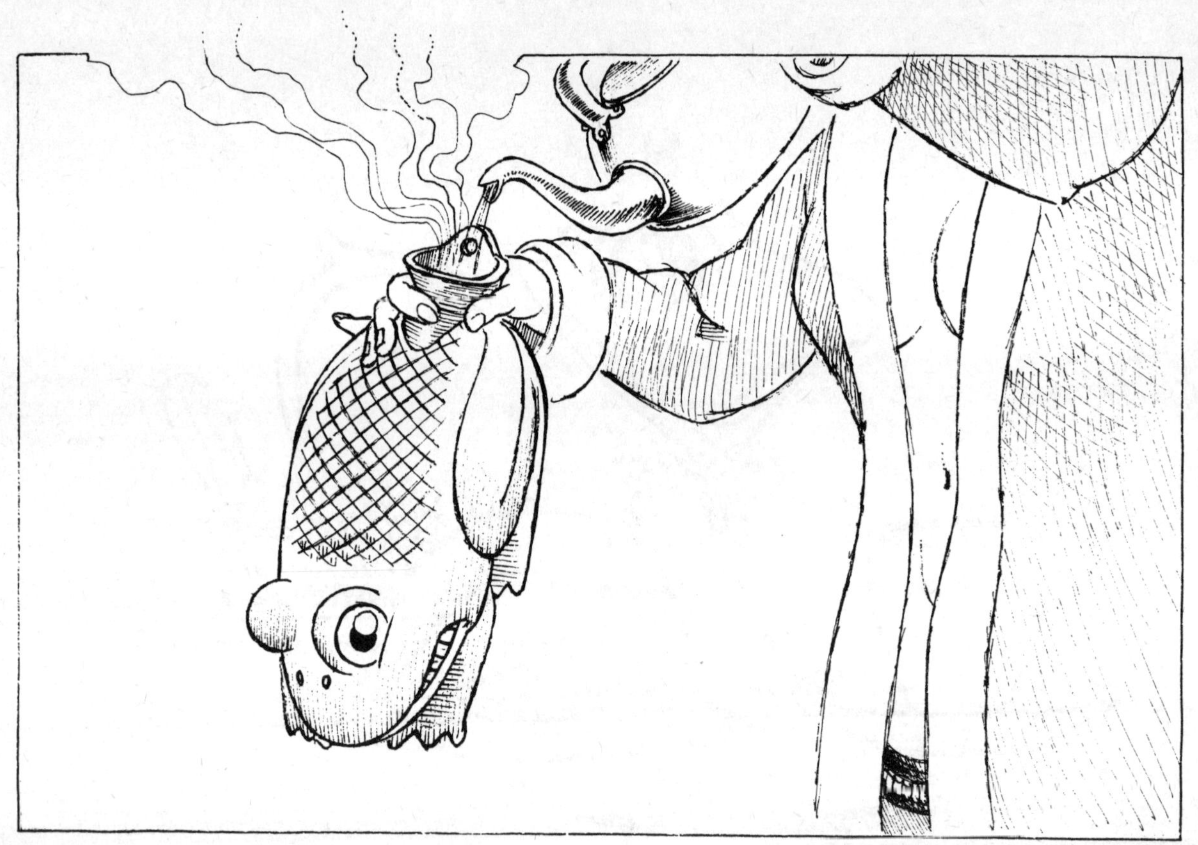

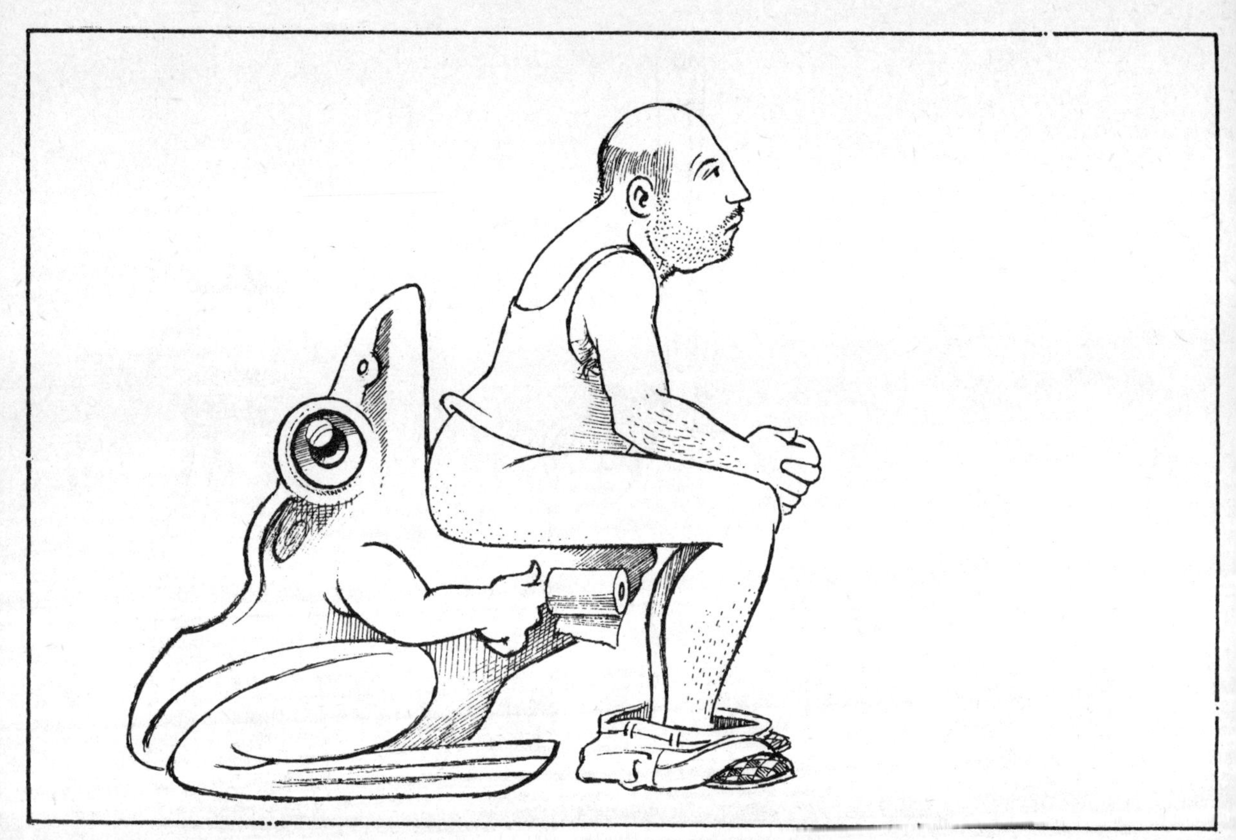

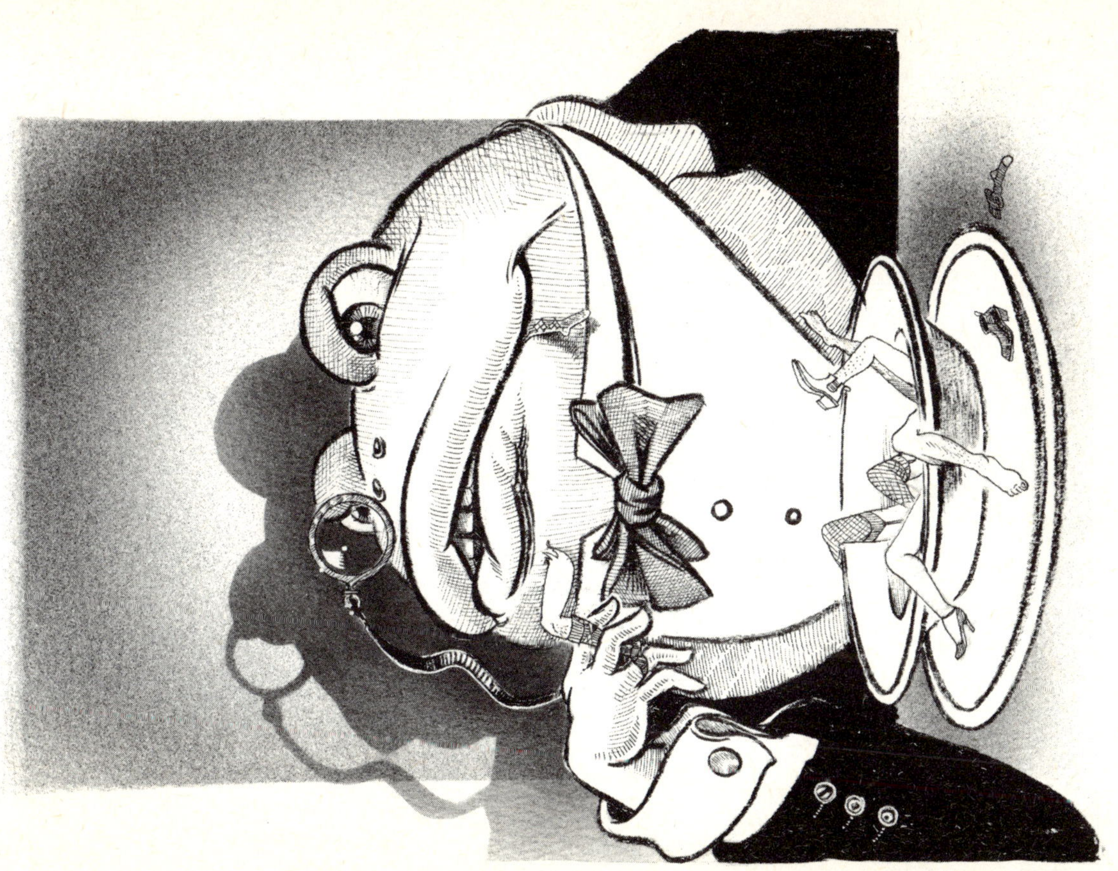

(Greensleeves ❖ Was ❖ My ❖ Delight)

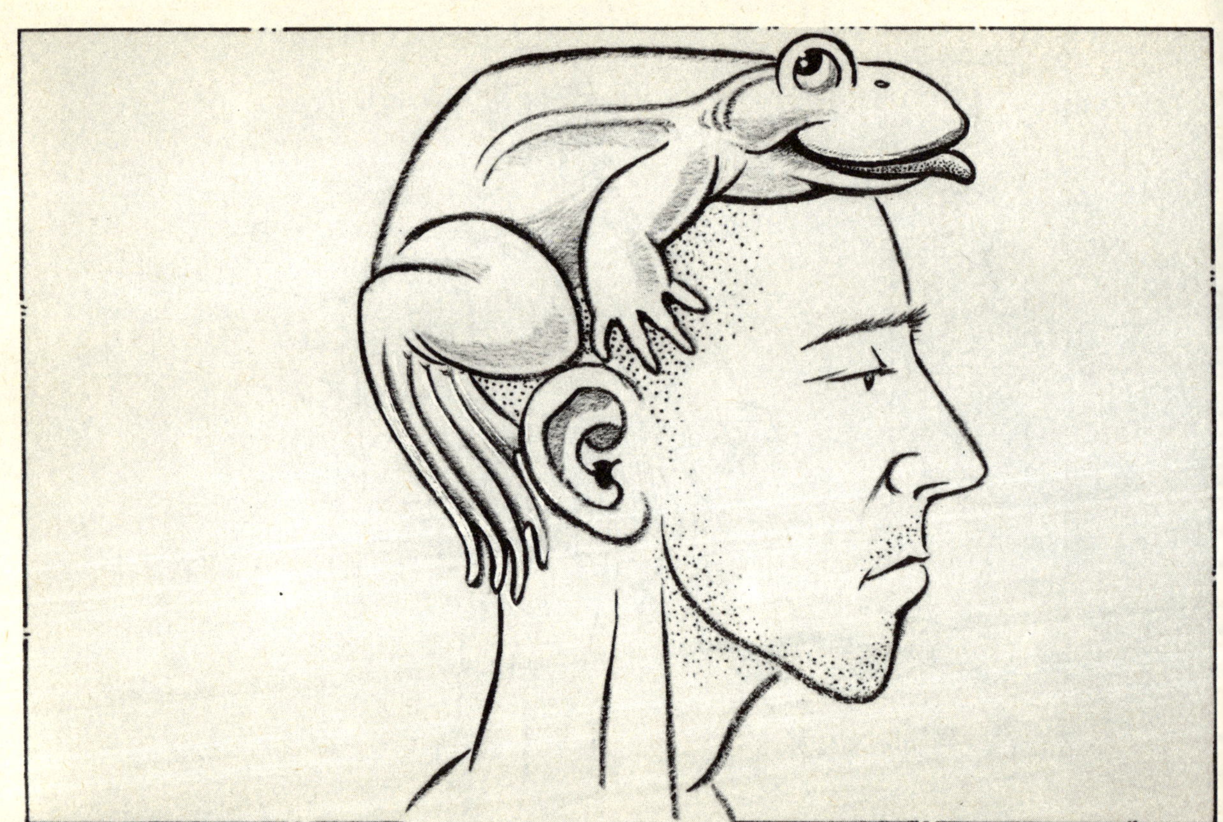

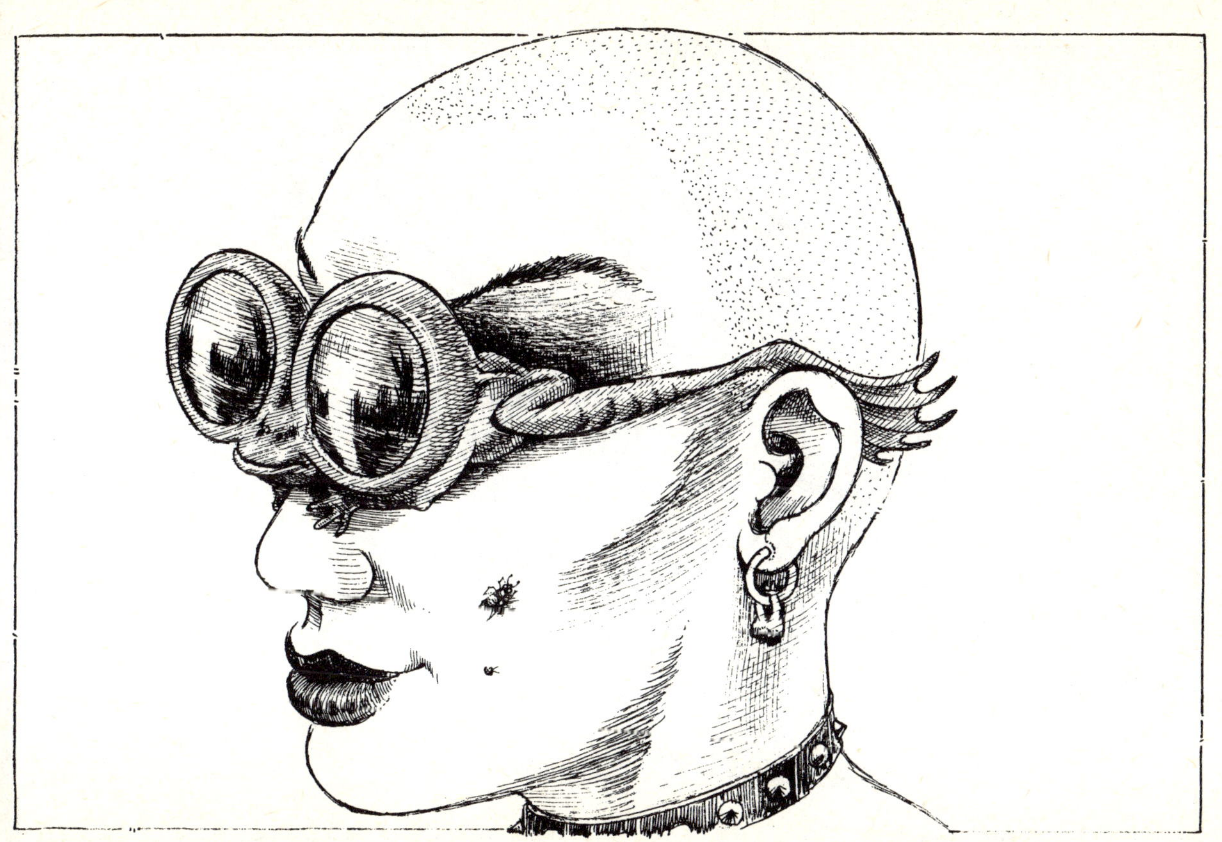

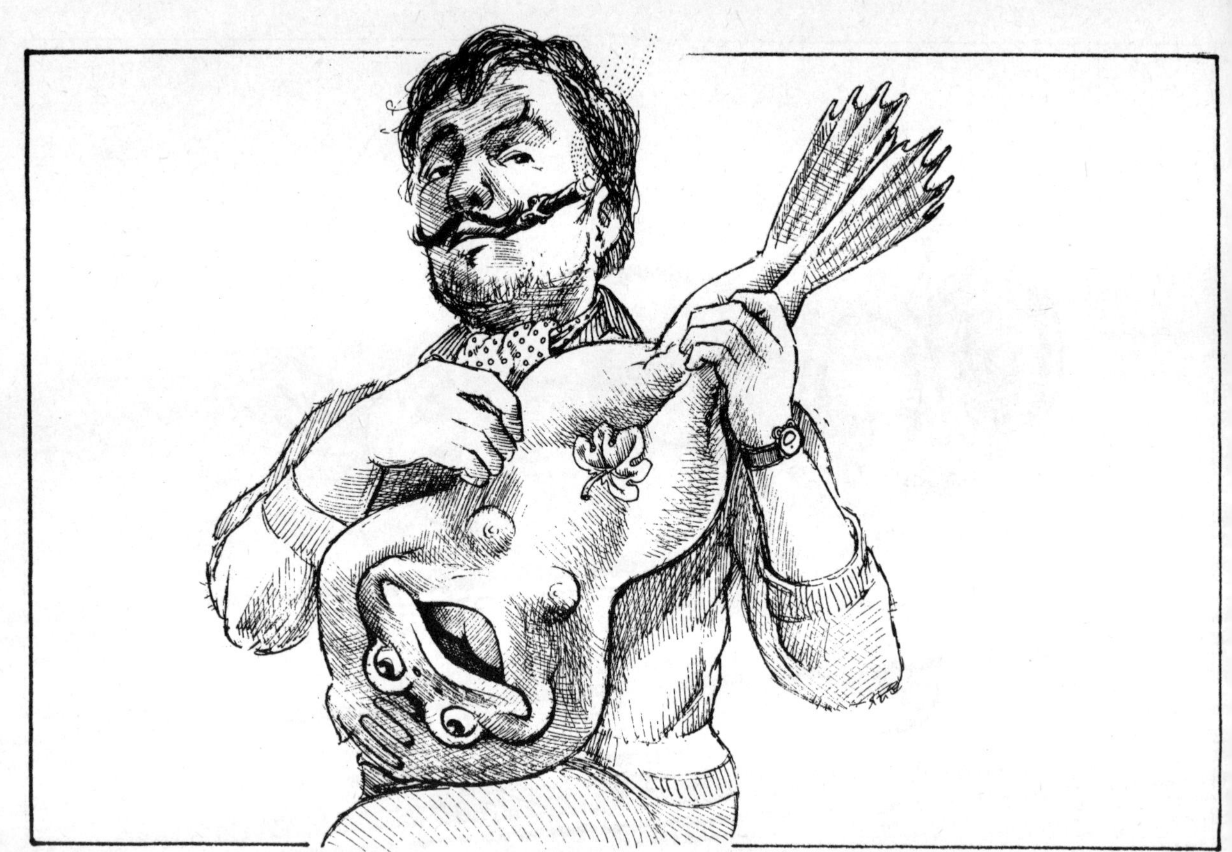

SUNBURY ON SEA
1
13

AERE

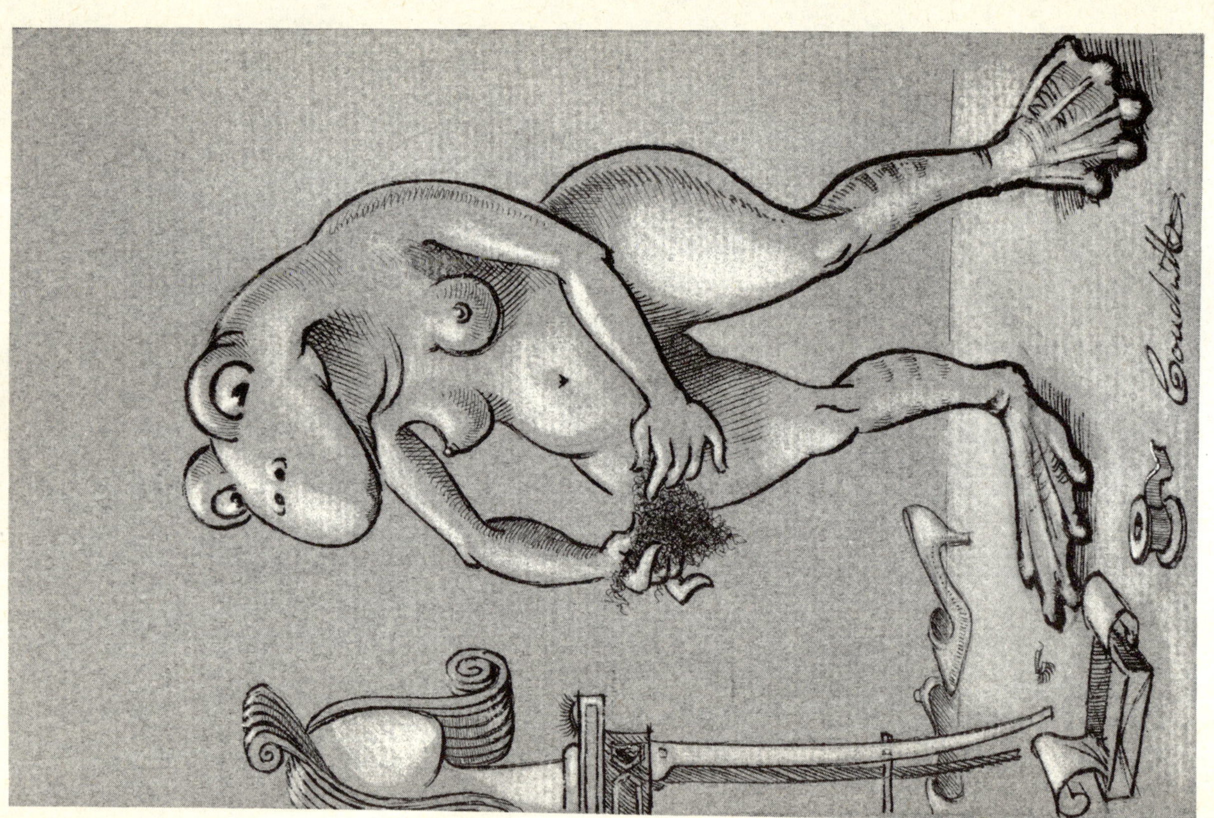

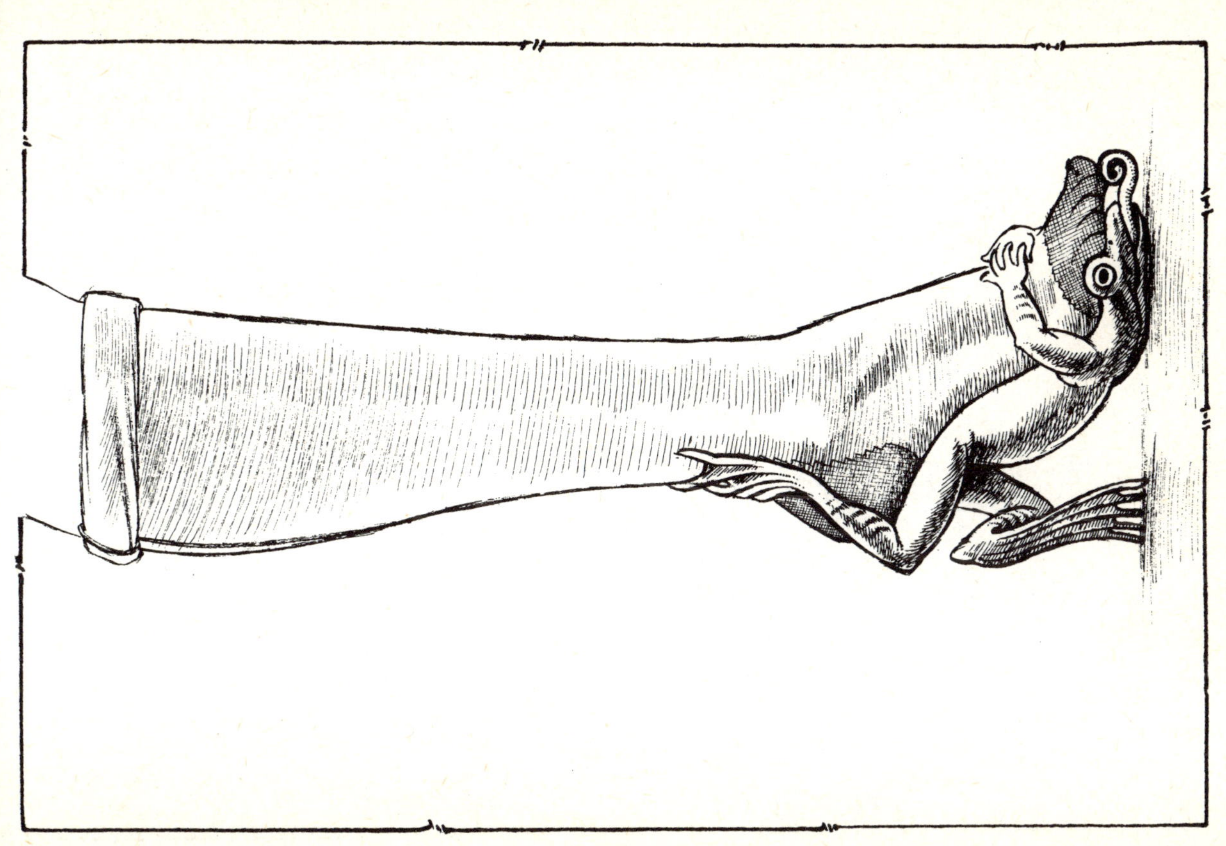

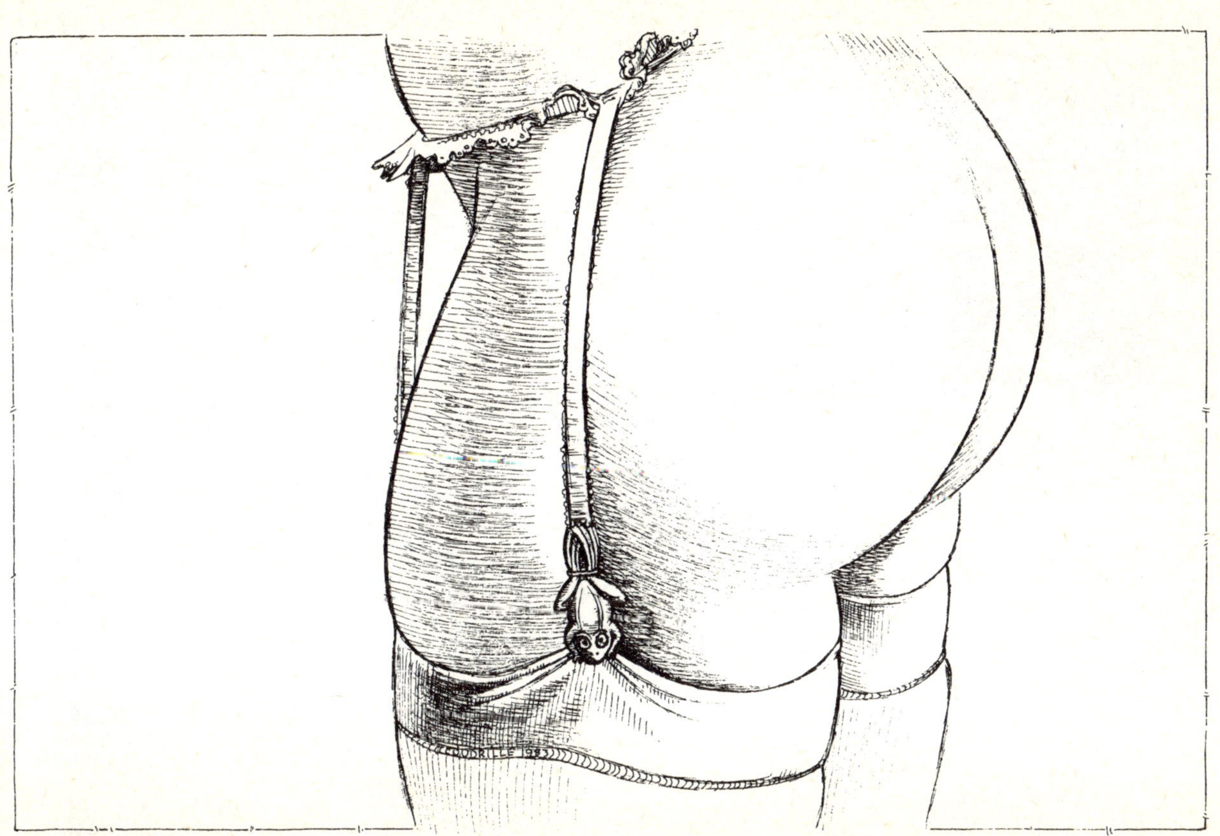
COUDRILLE 1983

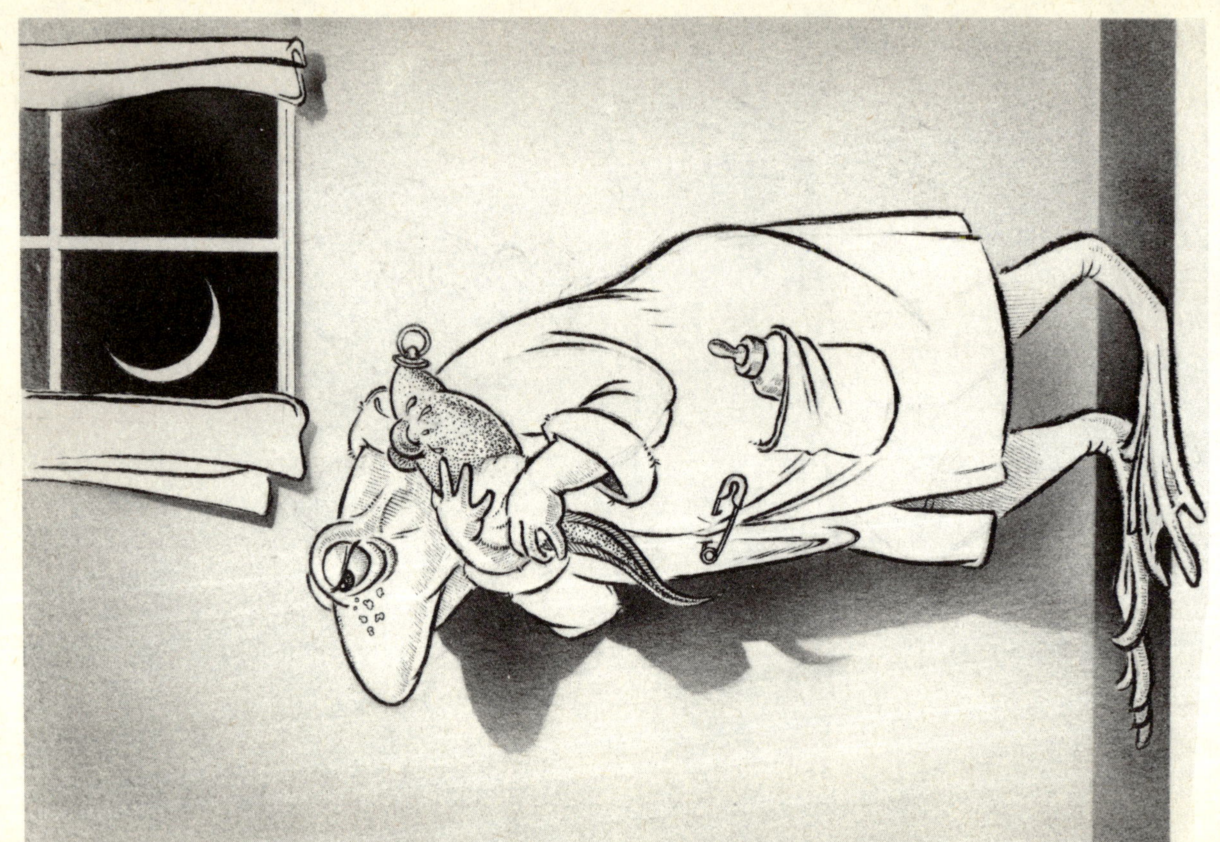

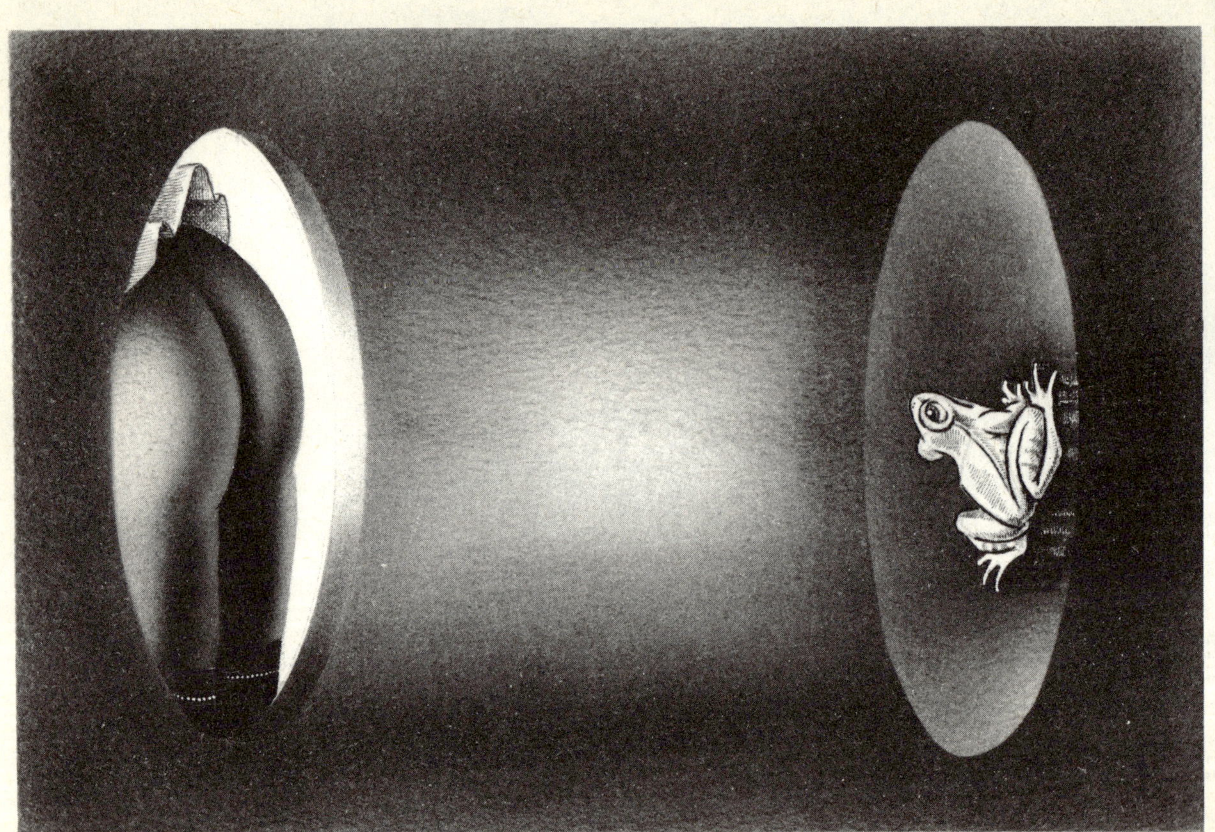

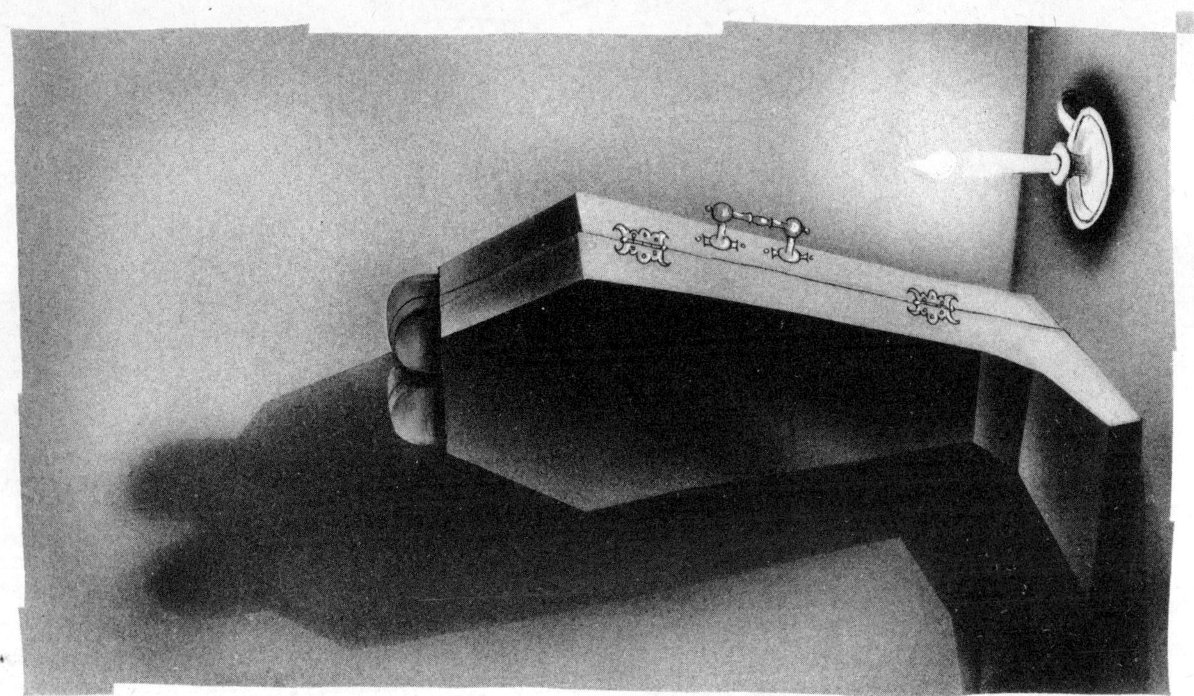